There Are No Shortcuts
In eCommerce Business.
(except these)

By

Christina E. Rogers

This booklet is dedicated to my Step Father in Heaven, Sulayman M. Jarra. There's not a day that I don't miss him. I hope he's proud.

My Mother. My heart. My angel. I love you.

My sister. My other half. I love you.

Alex. My constant. I love you.

Introduction

You know what they say!

"If I had someone tell me this before I did it, I wouldn't have done it!"

But that's not always the case. I'm a firm believer that experience is the absolute best teacher. I've lived my whole entire life ignoring the "warning" signs, "do not press this button" signs, "don't go this way" signs and "bitch, you're about to ruin your whole entire life" signs. Why is this? Because I'm a stubborn Taurus who's become even more stubborn by listening to her gut in every single situation in order to fulfill my life purpose even if it means jumping off of the metaphoric bridge of life. Let's face it, life is so gotdamn fun this way! Who wants to live the safe way? Who wants to watch for the eggshells so they won't step on them in fear that someone will hear it crack and point a finger while they step on their own eggshells?

    I always knew I had a bigger calling in life because I was that awkward little quiet kid at school who preferred to sit by herself and draw her future instead of be a kid! I didn't want to participate in sports, I didn't want to talk to anyone and I damn sure didn't want to go to class. My mom will co sign this along with the officer that was assigned to me who made sure I went to my High School classes after I got caught skipping school.

Right after High School, I went to Italy because I was a poor child who got sponsored to take the trip by a Community gem called Project Row Houses in Houston, TX. I went to Italy for $100!!! Now, if that's not destiny, what is? Anyway, I spent five weeks traveling with kids I grew to love and a group leader that impressed me by her ability to know so much Italian. In Italy, I realized that the world is so much bigger than you and I and even when I was on the other side of the world, not knowing a lick of Italian, I still found a way to communicate with aliens. *This* taught me how to break down the basic human *without* school, *without* a psychology class, *without* a college education and *without* professional training. I came up with this idea that out of all the books and information that's out there, someone must have experienced something in order to write the book. This is when it clicked to me that all I had to do was apply myself. The way that I gained my knowledge would be by my own means and ability and in my own time.

After Italy, I was supposed to go to college, and I did, but only for 2 semesters. The funniest part is that I went for two semesters, two different years for two weeks each. Comical. My grandfather tried to sit me down and tell me that I needed to go to college and that was the only reason I went back the second time but when I walked in the building, I felt my stomach turn every single time. It smelled like failure in there, it looked like dissatisfaction and it felt like High School. I gained so much knowledge in Italy that I didn't want to sell myself short by walking in that building ever again, so I dropped out. It was really that simple to make the decision!

Did I know what was going to happen next? No!

The beauty of the unknown has been my fuel for the past eleven years. I still don't know what's going to happen tomorrow and I wasn't aware that as we grew older we were given psychic powers. That's right, nobody knows what's going to happen next! That's why making the jump was easy. Either way, I wouldn't know what was going to happen but I did realize that one decision made me happier than the other, so I followed the decision that made me happiest. I'm a very spiritual person and I've learned that God wants His children to be happy. Sometimes it's difficult to hear the voice of

God, but if you are at peace with yourself, you understand which way to go by listening to your heart. God is inside of you and He leads you whether you think He does or not. But only if you're listening.

So after I dropped out of college, I got like a million jobs and I supported myself until I felt a pull in my spirit. I prayed one night and asked God to reveal my life story so I knew where to go. I dreamt it that night. He laid it out in front of me and I've been chasing it ever since. To make things more official, my best friend said she was moving to Los Angeles, CA within the next week and I said, "Well shit! I'm going too!"

I quit my job, I sold my stuff and I was excited about the land of the unknown… again!

Now I know why you're here and why you chose this booklet. It's because you want to take the shortcut to get where you want to go, but you have to realize that even if I give you all of this information, it's up to to you to take it to the next level! I could put the key of life right in the palm of your hands but if you don't use the key, it's pointless to have. Are you catchin' my drift? Good. Now, enough about me… let's talk business.

Brand Growth.

So you're wanting to grow your brand but you're standing there like a headless Hercules. You've got all that power, everything is set up and you have a customer base but you ain't got no head! You can't see where you're going and it feels like you're relying on the same people to buy your product. Basically, you need to grow your brand because more eyes equal more sales! Duh!

Now, one thing I've learned about growing my brand is that I absolutely need to understand my customer base and what they want and need in life. This means I have to get my hands dirty. I'd like to say that I have a good gauge on how to understand people in general. Before they even open their mouth, I already know what type of person it is and if we will mesh or not. This is based off of body language, what they choose to wear, how they walk, how they smile, etc... I'm pretty much the Inspector Gadget of personalities. I've always been this way, though. I've always observed everything around me. My mother can cosign this too because when I was a child and she lost her keys, I knew exactly where they were even if they were under a pile of clothes. #observant.

Figuring out your core audience will help you understand the millions of other people who are just like them. It will then help you understand the billions of people who are *not* like them. A few shortcuts to doing this are below.

Insights.

If you have an Instagram page that is linked to a business page on Facebook, you are well on your way to figuring out your customer base. The "insights" information tells you what percentage of males and females are following you, what age range is mostly following you, where most of them are located and when your followers are most active. This is very valuable information because it's literally telling you what type of people are interested in your products or general business and brand.

Ask Questions.

Don't be scared to talk to your customers and find out what they want from you or why they're there. Some customers are easy to figure out and others are quiet little lurkers who have private pages and don't let you see inside their world. The best way to figure them out is to get in contact with them. How do you get to know a friend of yours? You ask questions, watch how they react to certain situations and learn by experience that they don't like onions when they spit them out on the plate at dinner. This is how you have to treat your customers. Through my five year journey as an entrepreneur, I've learned about my customers by paying attention to every single thing that came across my screen. I know what they like, what they hate, what makes them happy, what pisses them off and what makes them spend. My suggestion is to post a question and wait for responses or actually email the customer with your questions.

How Do I Get My Instagram Poppin'?

This is such a broad question but I get it so often that I feel that I need to tell you. I'm going to say the same thing about your customer base or anyone who's interested in your brand or business idea. You need to learn them like the back of your hand. Even with that information, however, it's still a hit or miss. In my experience as an "Instagram Model" (thanks ShadeRoom! Also thank you to every other malicious and ill-intent human who wants to write me off), I've learned that you have to have the right angles, sis. You have to look like a million dollars to make that million dollars!

Let's face it. Instagram is all about visuals. I don't go on Instagram to read, unless I'm really intrigued by the photo. I go to scroll and look at all the stuff that I see before my eyes. Content is *everywhere* on Instagram and our brains don't care about it until we see something we like. **Point, blank, period.** Have you ever seen the transition of "Joanne The Scammer"? In the beginning, Branden Miller was just a normal guy posting on Instagram. Nothing spectacular was occurring that sparked our interests until one day, he posted a video portraying a white female who scams black men. This was funny as hell, we loved it, we shared it and we helped him deliver his baby, Joanne the Scammer. Branden took the most popular content and kept giving it to us because we loved it. It's that simple! It doesn't matter if you have a consistent 10 likes and then one day you have 150 likes or if you have a consistent 10,000 likes and then one day you have 200,000 likes. There's a spike there for a reason and your followers saw something in your content that made their heart rate jump. Use this method to determine how to get your Instagram poppin'.

    Also, please make sure you take the best photos possible. Save those blurry, horribly lit photos for the '80s. Thanks.

Save the boring stuff for the board meeting.

When your customers are looking to buy something or invest in your brand, they're not looking be bored doing it. They also don't want to be told what to do. They'd prefer to accidentally purchase a lot of stuff that they'll brag about to their friends later. Target has this method. When you walk in Target it's like a big playground for adults. There's so much fun stuff and I get distracted and accidentally buy a grass thing that has a deer antler attached to it because everyone needs one, right? So basically, you have to make your brand intriguing to the customer. Make them feel like they're having fun. For example, Susan wants to sell ice cream. We've had ice cream before but we haven't had Susan's ice cream and the way she holds her ice cream in front of the scariest jungle animals makes us intrigued by her ice cream. It makes us look a little further into what's going on with this ice cream. Now let's look at Sandra. Sandra sells ice cream, too. We've had ice cream before, but we haven't had Sandra's ice cream and the way she posts the ice cream bucket makes us wonder what the next post has to offer.

I learned something about humans. They like to have a little sneaky fun every now and then. Whether it be doing something naughty like having an extra glass of wine when you weren't supposed to or something like cheating on your pregnant girlfriend and ending up all over TMZ… too soon? Anyway, if you use this method to sell, you're getting in touch with your customers emotions. Use fun captions to sell your brand to someone. For example, don't just say, **"Buy this now."** because, **"We won't tell your boyfriend you bought this."** sounds like so much fun!

Do your own thing.

Over the years I've been tagged in several pictures of mine that other clothing boutiques use to sell their products. All I do now is shake my head, but my initial feeling is, "That's so wack!" You don't want to be that guy! You're an entrepreneur for a reason and you started your brand for a reason.

brand
brand/
noun
noun: **brand**; plural noun: **brands**
   1   **1**.
        a type of product manufactured by a particular company under a particular name.

So even though Shop Chriss Zoë is a boutique, my brand is Chriss Zoë. People associate Chriss Zoë with my entrepreneurship journey among whatever else they associate with my name. I've built my brand solely off of the things that I wanted to be associated with when someone hears my name or I introduce myself to them. This is why branding yourself with your own ideas is so important. The easy work will definitely keep your business at a standstill because you'll always be grabbing from someone else's hard work. Create your own logo, create your own feel and create your own method of running your business and brand. It creates longevity in your journey and it allows people to tell you apart from other brands.

The Easiest eCommerce Life.

When I first started my store, I feel like everything I did was manual labor. I mean, it was like the 1960 to our 2018. I would go to the Los Angeles Fashion District and walk in every store I thought had potential for my brand, pick out outfits that I thought looked nice, lugged that heavy shit back to my car, go back for more, go home, get cute, stand in front of a tripod, take pictures, edit them, post them up, get sales, wake up the next morning and do the packages, insert tracking numbers, customer emails, take a trip to the post office and go home and pass out. That wasn't even half of what I needed to do to grow my brand because there was still the marketing aspect and the accounting aspect and everything else in between. Chile, in short, it was difficult to get the store where it is today so when I see the strides that are being taken to ensure new boutique owners and seasoned boutique owners alike are given the easiest eCommerce experience ever, I'm not only pissed that it didn't happen sooner but I'm also not dumb enough to not jump on the opportunity. These tips below will help you understand what I mean.

Dropshipping is a fucking gift from God.

In my previous rant, I described all it took for me to get a package out the door and into the hands of my eager customer. That was a whole two days of work and effort but now there are options like dropshipping which make it *so much easier* to be a boutique owner. If you're reading this booklet for a different reason and don't care about dropshipping, skip this section. Now I know I said don't use other people's vision to shape your brand, but ignore that for this section because I have a good way to still make it your own brand. Proceed.

    Dropshipping was created by the most intelligent man or woman on the planet and I only say this because I'm very grateful for the concept. Don't know what dropshipping is? Well, wholesalers got smart (or whoever it was) and bought a whole bunch of product, shot the product and offered it to the buyers as a "non bulk" situation. Instead of spending a lot of cash upfront, dropshippers make it easy for you to just choose what you want to put on your store and sell.

Once your customer buys the product, all you do is order it from the dropshipper and they do the rest. I'm serious. You're literally getting paid to do nothing but buy something that someone else bought from you. I should be pissed off even more that you guys get it so easy, but I'm grateful that you have it easy because I wouldn't want you to struggle like I did.

Now, the way you find these dropshippers is the work you put in to find them. I can't give you all the good secrets, sis or bruh. Any good businesswoman knows to keep it right and keep it tight. *Dim the lights and lower the kites.*

USPS picks up packages for crying out loud!

So I was crossing over into my "$40,000 a month life" and found myself dropping off at least 6 bags of packages to the post office every single day. It got to the point where I went to the post office one morning and a gentleman said, **"You drop off everyday, huh?"** I can't front, I was embarrassed. Sometimes I struggled to drop those packages off and other times I had help, but the mere thought of someone witnessing me drop off packages through rain, sleet, snow, tears, sweat, blood and beer bellies had me feeling a little embarrassed. So I respond to the guy of course and he then proceeds to tell me how USPS can actually come to your house or warehouse and get your shipments for you so you don't have to look like you just played a basketball game after you got caught cheating on a pregnant Khloe Kardashian. Sorry, I couldn't resist. So yeah, reason number two that I should be pissed off that you guys get to run your business easier than I did previously.

Shopify.

If you have my booklet, "How I Became My Own Business", you know that I'm a hardcore fan of Shopify. I literally should have an endorsement with Shopify because I rant on and on about how awesome they are but I'm sure so many other people do that, too, so I'm no different. Anyway, Shopify made it so easy to run an eCommerce business.

By the way, a random fact about Shopify is that a few guys started it because they couldn't find a good hosting site for their snowboarding company in 2004. By 2006, Shopify was launched and by 2018, the owners are billionaires. Like, shoot me now.

So anyway, the idea is perfect because now it gives entrepreneurs a chance to thrive and now big companies like Target who's been around forever are probably pissed about this just how I'm pissed about you having it easy. So yeah, Shopify makes it so that you can have a bangin' website, they basically give you all the tools for success with their long list of apps that run your store for you and it's only about $30 a month to own your spot on Shopify. Don't get it confused because the apps do cost money, but it's well worth your while. Trust me.

Make dropshipping your own if necessary.

Since dropshipping is made to make your life easier, there seems to be that dull space where you feel that you don't have to do extra work. You do, though. To enhance your dropshipping experience while you're growing your business, order what you put on your store, shoot it and put those pictures in the place of the stock photos. Boom. A whole separate level to this! Take caution, however, because since dropshipping is offered to plenty of others, the clothing might sell out quickly, leaving you with lots of photos and no product.

Let's Talk About Employees

Now, for the longest time I was doing this all by myself. I'm not kidding. I built my business with $200 and helped it grow legs so it could make it to a six-figure business but I did it single-handedly. Throughout the years I've had some pretty incredible friends and associates. I've been in contact with the richest people I've ever known and I've gotten advice from them that helped me make my business decisions. All these business people usually told me that my car was a waste of money but I ignored every single one of them because my Range Rover, *I call him Marco Cuban*, makes me so fucking happy and he makes me work harder and there's nothing anyone can do to tear us apart, unless your name is Porsche Macan or Lamborghini Urus. Now, even though I ignored that advice, I took a lot of advice which made my life much easier. I put a few gems below. You didn't hear this from me, though.

"Hire someone you stubborn little girl!"

I used to complain about the pain in my back, how I never had time to do anything, how I was stressed out, how work felt like punishment and the list goes on. So I fell into this cycle of complaining until one day someone simply said, **"Take the financial L and hire someone."** I remember it like yesterday. I honestly didn't want to hire anyone because I didn't trust anyone with my baby, but that was the dumbest thing I could have committed to. So, I remember my eyes tearing up because I was fighting with myself about actually hiring someone and he's sitting across from me watching this whole mental tug of war and asks me what's on my mind. I told him how I felt and he said that I can't do it alone and in order to make my business grow, I need to hire someone.

Of course this is me in year 5 of my six-figure business with $40,000 a month in sales but I can't help to think how beneficial it still would have been if it were earlier.

My first day as a free woman, I wondered where all of my goals and future plans went because I actually had nothing to do. The transition to get my business handed over to others was tough, but I did it and it's being done now but the reward is so great.

I no longer stress out everyday, I have a clear mind that's able to start working on other ideas that will eventually grow big enough to be handed over to other employees and I sit back in gratitude every single day which allows a healthy exchange from me to the universe.

I remember listening to a podcast and the young woman said, **"It's so easy to make a million dollars! You just have to have multiple streams of income and lots of help."**

Turns out, I had been getting hints for months before I actually hired people. Basically, I wouldn't try to do everything on my own anymore because when people help you, it's so much pressure off of my mind, body and soul.

"Communicate with your employees thoroughly."

So, here I am. I'm an official boss. Now I need to learn how to actually *lead* my employees the proper way. I thought I did everything I was supposed to do as a boss. I let everyone know what needed to be done and I went about my day. *Wrong.* **Micromanaging is not what it is. Communication is what it is.** I always felt guilty about standing over someone's shoulder and watching their every move, but I also had a different definition and idea of what it actually was. Being detailed with my employees is very important to the success of my business. I had to learn that if I didn't communicate exactly what I wanted, it wouldn't get done. *PERIOD.*

Now, when I explain something to an employee, I am sure to map out exactly what I mean, want and require so that there's a higher chance of it getting done than not. The reality is that an employee needs to be taught what the overall vision of the company is so that they might comply with the instructions and play a legit role in helping the company achieve that goal of success. If I don't communicate that, there's no way it will get done since I didn't hire mind readers. Where do those get hired by the way? I may need to hire a few.

Business Tools

I realize that some shit may be expensive but I believe that the effort you put into your business will show. There are things that you need to clearly survive in this business world. There's so many gadgets and apps that can help you run a business in your living room and they're so important to the growth of your business. I know this, because I grew my business in my bedroom, which eventually turned into growing my business in the living room, which eventually turned into growing my business in my office.

Spending money when you aren't sure you're going to get it back is hard. Trust me, I know. Guess what it is though? It's called having faith in yourself. Remember when I said I didn't know what would happen next after I left college? Well, I didn't. I just quit. I had faith that whatever happened would be for my own good. Some people will quit college and wish on a star and that pretty much shapes up their lives, but if you work hard and stay focused, you're going to get where you deserve to be.

Below are a few things that I absolutely needed to run and sustain my business. Happy hour can wait, you have big dreams!

A laptop.

It is 2018. If you don't have a working laptop and you're an entrepreneur, just come and give me a hug and let's start over. A laptop is extremely important because you need to be able to access your business wherever you are. I rarely go anywhere without my laptop these days because I'm so hands on with building my business up and there are multiple things that I can't do without a laptop. I know what you're thinking. A laptop is so expensive. A laptop will run you about $1300 and that's only a dream and a budget away. Don't get flustered, you can do it.

Social Media.

Face it. Social media runs the world and that's just the reality of it all. There have been so many successful influencers that I'm wondering why people even go to college anymore. If you do not have social media, you need to create an Instagram, Twitter, Facebook, Snapchat, etc… You need a social media presence to get your brand out there because if nobody sees your brand, nobody will buy into it. Many people don't understand how important and crucial one like or comment can be to your brand. Let's say my name is Janet and I have 3 million followers on Instagram. I'm scrolling along and I see a post from your business page. I know a lot of people don't follow you, but I'm supporting your business because you're my friend.

    I like your picture and comment, "Wow, this is dope!"

    I then continue scrolling and scrolling and eventually forget I even commented on your picture. I just gave you access to my 3 million followers by commenting on and liking your picture. There are many useful tools on Instagram that make it so easy to grow your business or be seen.

There's a section that allows your followers to see what you're liking and commenting on and there's also a section that shows you what's popular in your "general circle of friends." These people are the people who may or may not like the same things you like, may have clicked on the same stuff as you and may just accidentally clicked on the same thing you clicked on. Everything on Instagram is linked together and since Facebook is buying out all these social media platforms, everything is starting to operate the same way! *So in short, get a damn social media life!*

"Mentors".

When I say this, I mean like-minded individuals who have the same goals and aspirations as you and it doesn't matter what level they're on in their life. I learned so much by the people I surrounded myself with throughout the years. I genuinely created relationships with them and along the way they taught me little things that helped me tremendously.

If you're around people who constantly want to do things that are not beneficial for your life, guess what? You guessed it. You'll be doing the same thing in the same cycle for the same amount of years it could've taken you to get started the first time.

One thing about my friends is that they hate spending the night with me places. I wake up at the crack of dawn almost every single day. Once I wake up, I wake the house up because I'm in work mode and no matter how quiet I try to be, I can't help but to randomly drop my computer which starts a domino effect and knocks down everything in the room as I stand there with a shocked look on my face.

    Neither here nor there, I've noticed that the house naturally wakes up earlier because I wake up earlier. If there are constant habits around you, as a human, you are almost positively going to do the same thing because we thrive off of the "Monkey See, Monkey Do" lifestyle. You can say that you march to the beat of your drum all day, but if your whole group of friends takes a shot of Tequila at a day party with the music blasting, you will too.

Find you some folks who will elevate your life and make sure you learn all you can from them. Be careful not to become a leech, though. Nobody likes those.

Some Spiritual Stuff

I am a really big believer in the spiritual world and the universe. Everyone around me is, too. Those who aren't into the spiritual world but end up in our group of friends eventually cave in and become apart of the spiritual world. Part of my success comes from the work I dedicate myself to, but the other part comes from using my mind to control a lot of things (*without saying it, which I must say or it may get misconstrued, God is the whole entire reason for my success.*). I've had this debate with a friend of mine who I'm convinced just likes to argue and debate because he challenges everything I say and everything everyone else says, but anyway, he thinks that we don't control what happens in our future.

I agree because we aren't sure what's going to happen next, but I disagree because we choose the paths we're going down and we attract a lot of things that come our way. Controlling the mind is an exercise that must be used often and must be used daily to get the maximum result. The most important thing about controlling the mind is already believing that whatever it is has happened. Once you start living out your dreams mentally, you're attracting those dreams to you. They want to meet you! *The mind is powerful.*

    I always play this playlist in my car called, "Wine Ya Waist" and I have a favorite song on that list called, "FIA" by Davido. Sometimes when I'm riding along in good spirits, I'll think to myself, *"I hope "FIA" is next."* and when it actually comes on I get a little shook until I realize that I should be singing along. Coincidence or brain power?

The other day, I was in the gym and I tried to move a stability ball with my energy, but it didn't work. Don't tell anyone that. I just thought I'd confess that I take it a little too far sometimes.

Once you gain control over your brain power, you're able to conquer your biggest goals and aspirations. I once wrote myself a check for $100,000 hoping to make that amount in a year. I'm not sure why I picked such a small number, but I did. Anyhow, I was minding my business one day and I randomly checked my analytics on Shopify. $103k in three months. I kept my head down and worked but surely didn't think that I'd reach my goal in that short period of time. At the same exact time, my sister found herself in my bank account and told me I had reached a personal goal of mine.

My heart was filled with gratitude. I even remember saying, "I love my life!" while staring outside of the window for a short period of time. I sent out the most positive vibrations that I didn't even realize I was sending out. Everyday after that has been amazing and I've sent out the same gratitude to the universe not because I know it will keep taking care of me, but because I'm truly grateful. So grateful that I sometimes find myself with tears streaming down my face in disbelief that this is actually my life.

So, not to get all mushy on you guys, but I know for a fact that a life without limits is a limitless life, obviously. That speaks volumes. Tips on *"spiritual stuff"* are below. Please keep in mind that this is not a light subject and if you honestly want to take this journey, it takes patience, practice and persistence.

Gratitude.

- Take gratitude walks
- Say "thank you" to the universe
- Operate at a high vibration when you're being grateful

Believe.

- Believe in your dreams 100%
- Believe in your vision so much that it's already happening to you.
- No matter how silly, speak your goals and dreams

Research.

- Daily devotionals help keep you on track. Use it as research towards a healthy spirit.
- Find people who are in the spiritual practice and listen to what they have to say.
- There's plenty of books and articles that help you understand the universe and how it wants to help you.

Some Unsolicited Advice

(or maybe it is solicited since you bought this book)

Take a Break.

Being an entrepreneur or business owner or whatever you want to label yourself as is hard as hell. The days can start slow and end like you're the fucking President of the United States. Every single day is a mystery and you'll never know how successful you will be for the day because it's all up in the air.

The easiest thing about going to a normal job is that you're guaranteed that check and the end of the pay period and it doesn't matter if you go to work and work hard or go to work and don't work at all. You don't feel the stress of what's going on behind the scenes at all.

As an entrepreneur, if you don't work, you don't eat. If you don't work, your business is stagnant. Are you catching my drift? My advice during tough days is to take a break. The universe has a funny way of letting you know when the high tide is. I say this because I've experienced it over and over again. If it's just not my day and nothing is going the way I planned it, I sit down and take a deep breath. I'll take the day off and take in the beauty of the world until I catch my vibe and then I'll go back to work with an open mind and better energy.

A positive workspace is the most rewarding way to work. Everything just flows with ease and just the way it's supposed to.

Do it yourself.

There's a thin line between asking for help and just being plain annoying. I hate when people ask me stuff that's a Google search away. I hate it because they would rather put that burden on me than do the research themselves. I've always been a "search and find" type of person and before I ask someone for help I try to at least do it myself. This way, I've managed to save tons of money and if everyone I hired to run my business were to walk away today, I'd still be able to sustain my business because I learned how to do it myself first.

Your worst bet is depending on someone else. This is never a good way to live your life even. I know y'all saw "Diary of A Mad Black Woman"! If you learn the ropes yourself, you won't have to depend on another soul to help you flourish because you already know how to do it and Lil Boosie even spelled it out for us! I-N-D-E-P-E-N-D-E-N-T, do you know what I mean?

Invest in your Manifest.

You have to manifest first. Dream so big that you feel it when you walk and talk and all that energy will pull it into reality through the work that you do. Dream/vision boards are important to have. You literally sit there and think about what you want in your future and then you post it in a place where you will see it everyday and you actually think about it everytime you see it. Believe that it will happen, and it will.

Investing in books is a sure way to gain knowledge on this lifestyle. Every successful person can tell you how they got to their success, but every successful person can't tell you the same story. The truth is that everyone has different paths, but the paths that came before yours will always lead you in the right direction unless you're trying to be the first astronaut to text Obama in space and sell Flat Tummy Tea from the smallest laptop. I still support you if you're wanting to step off the beaten path and I believe that it's great for you! Do it with confidence and focus and you will be sure to be successful.

Outro

Alright kiddos, I hope you enjoyed this booklet and I hope that you got something from it. I try my best to use the blood, sweat and tears and turn them into a Margarita for those who ask. I hope your journey is amazing and I wish you the most success. Thank you for supporting me in every avenue and God Bless You!

- Chriss

Acknowledgments

I would be nothing without the great God on my side. I am thankful for His grace and mercy throughout my life and I am grateful for every idea, hurdle conquered and journey that I've endured for I know that it would not be possible without Him.

My mother is an angel and I've learned so much from her that I might as well hand every award won her way. She is the purest form of a vessel that leads and guides me through life effortlessly. A selfless and beautiful creature.

My sister is just a badass. She's my best friend and my road dog through this life. I'm so grateful because she's taught me a lot about business as well and

I wouldn't have even started this journey if it weren't for her.

To all of my rich ass friends who gave me advice throughout the years, thank you.

To all those rich ass associates who had me around their worldly possessions, thank you. That motivated me to do boss things out of competitiveness.

To all those people who ever decided to become friends with the devil and played your cards against me, thank you. You motivated me with that shit.

To everyone who allows me to be me, I thank you. That is the truest gift a human can ever give me. I love you.

Remember to love your neighbor and your brother and sister. God wants His children to survive and be treated with love and respect.

Chriss.

Made in the USA
Columbia, SC
08 August 2018